the Twelve Voices of Easter

by Woodrow Kroll

BACK TO THE BIBLE
Lincoln, Nebraska 68501

10,000 printed to date—1995
(1150-111-10M-35)
ISBN 0-8474-1460-4

Cover Design and Illustrations by Robert Greuter & Associates

Printed in the United States of America.

CONTENTS

Judas

VOICE OF BETRAYAL
Matthew 26:14-16, 47-50, 27:3-5

*J*esus chose Judas to be one of the Twelve. He became the treasurer for a band of men considered Christ's most trusted friends and companions. He was an intimate part of a group privileged to occupy the front-row seats for every miracle and teaching. Yet Judas betrayed him. "Traitor" is an ugly name, but it fit him well. There have been men like Judas before, and there will be again, but none will be remembered or despised as much as he.

Here I stand at the edge of this cliff, a rope around my neck. The other end is attached to that limb. How did I get myself into such a mess? What brought me to this desperate act?

I know now that I was a tool of Satan. He entered my heart and mind and completely controlled me. I was willing to do anything he wanted me to do. I know, too, that I was a pawn of the religious leaders. They searched relentlessly for an opportunity to arrest Jesus without creating a riot. I gave them that opportunity.

You see, I wanted to hurt Jesus more than anyone else. Why? Because He treated me with such unreasonable compassion. His eyes reflected it every time our money pouch came up short of cash. Jesus knew I was stealing. He knew how selfish and critical I was, always more concerned about myself than others. Still, He treated me with kindness. I was ashamed; out of that shame came hatred, hatred that brought me to this tree and to this cliff.

But don't get me wrong. I'm not here because of the members of the Sanhedrin or the other religious leaders. They don't care whether I live or die. They paid me my thirty pieces of silver, so I'm no longer any concern of theirs. Nor am I here because Satan made me come. He's probably glad to see me die; still it doesn't matter. I know who's to blame. They all used me, but I alone am responsible for this rope around my neck.

What brought the situation to a head was the Passover meal. We disciples met in an upper room with Jesus for this solemn observance. Most of our conversation around the table concerned the festivities of the next seven days. Occasionally someone would complain about the Romans and their threat to our way of life, but mostly we talked of love and loyalty to Jehovah. I could hardly stand it.

Suddenly, Jesus interrupted our conversation and announced that one of us would betray Him. You could have heard a pin drop. We looked at each other, stunned, and one by one began to ask, "Is it I, Lord?" Jesus said the one dipping his bread in the dish with Him at that moment was the betrayer. All eyes turned toward me; my hand was in the dish. I hastily withdrew it, but it didn't make any difference. Everyone knew I was the one, but no one said a word.

My anger flared. I had hidden my hatred for Him for so many months, and now He exposed it in a moment's time to everyone. I had already been to the chief priests with a plan to betray Him. They were more than happy to accept my offer. I'm sure Peter and John and the rest of them didn't know about the deal I made, but Jesus did.

Again His eyes met mine as He announced my intentions. I couldn't believe He still looked at me so kindly. Why didn't He denounce me? Why didn't He hit me? That I could understand. But this unwavering love for me—that was beyond my comprehension.

I needed to get out of there. Indignantly, as if to deny my plans for betrayal, I stood to my feet and rushed out of the room. I went directly to the chief priests and told them they must hurry. Once my treachery became known, the word would spread through the city. "We must act now," I said. They agreed.

Together we went to Pilate to request a detachment of Roman soldiers to accompany us to Gethsemane because we thought Jesus' disciples might put up a fight. Pilate was reluctant to grant our request, but he did. For that matter, I wasn't even sure Jesus would be in the garden, but it was a favorite gathering place for His disciples and Him. He loved to go there and pray in the peace and solitude of the olive trees.

We wound our way through the narrow streets under the cover of darkness—the Roman soldiers, the Jewish temple guard, the chief priests and elders, all led by me. By now my hatred had turned to fear. What if something went wrong?

When we arrived at Gethsemane there He was, praying. He appeared at first to be alone. Then I noticed some huddled shapes at His feet. Apparently His disciples had fallen asleep, and He was just rousing them when we arrived.

I stepped forward from the shadows. I was eager to get it over with. Our torches did not provide much light, so I had prearranged a sign that would identify Jesus in the darkness. As I think back on it now, I realize how cruel and treacherous this signal was. I kissed Him on the cheek and

called Him "Rabbi." Somehow I feel that generations from now many people will likely recoil in horror and anger at what I did. I betrayed the Lord with a kiss.

So here I am, standing at the edge of this cliff. I have been a coward from the start, and now I'm trying to muster enough courage for this last act of cowardice. If only I could look into His eyes once more and see the compassion and forgiveness there, but it's too late.

Peter

VOICE OF DENIAL
Matthew 26:32-35, 57-58, 69-75

*P*eter wept bitterly. His hands, roughened by sea water and fish nets, covered his tear–stained face and muffled his sobs. He was the one who had confidently declared, "Even if all are made to stumble because of you, I will never be made to stumble." Yet as the Easter story unfolded, he did exactly that. How could he have denied his Lord not once, not twice, but three times? His only hope was that some day he might declare his true feelings about Jesus.

How I hated hearing that rooster crow. Its penetrating cry pierced my heart. Oh sure, I had heard roosters crow many times before. I'm a fisherman. Almost all of my life I have fished the Galilee during the night. At daybreak, when it was time to bring our catch to shore, I often heard the roosters crowing. Yet no cock ever crowed with the shrillness or intensity of this one. I felt devastated when I heard it.

Jesus warned me. He said Satan would sift me as a farmer sifts his wheat. The Savior also said He had prayed for me, that my faith would not completely fail. Yet He knew I would deny Him when the time came.

How could this happen? Just hours ago I defended my Savior in the Garden of Gethsemane. Impulsively, I attempted to keep the soldiers from apprehending Him by drawing my sword and attacking Malchus, one of the servants of the high priest. How could such an act of bravery be followed by such an act of cowardice? I'll be asking myself that for a long time.

I remember the confusion when they led Jesus away from the garden. Most of the disciples scattered in fear, but John and I followed the mob to the palace of the high priest. I don't know exactly what drew us there. Maybe we felt compelled to find out what would happen to Jesus.

The high priest's house was on the other side of Jerusalem. We made our way through the dark streets, staying a safe distance behind the soldiers. The high priest is one of the wealthiest citizens in Jerusalem, and his house shows it. It is a palatial home with the rooms built around an open courtyard. To get to the inner courtyard we had to pass through an arched passageway. The opening from the street was blocked by a heavy gate. Another gate at the other end of the passageway barred our entrance to the courtyard. A young lady served as a gatekeeper. Fortunately, she knew John, so when he hastily said to her, "He's with me. Let us in," she did. We were inside the high priest's house.

John followed the soldiers to the hall, where a large crowd had assembled. I thought it best to mingle with those milling around. I wanted to melt into the crowd. What if someone recognized me? I had just cut off the ear of the high priest's servant. Surely one of these men would remember me. It was dangerous for me to be here, but where else should I go?

Suddenly, the young girl who sat at the gate came over to where I was warming myself by the fire. I knew she was uneasy when John asked her to admit both of us to the courtyard.

"You're one of this man's disciples, aren't you?" To say yes would have been asking for trouble, so I denied it. "Not me! I'm not a follower of the Nazarene." I turned my back to her and began to talk with some of the men gathered around the fire. I wanted her to go away. Eventually she did, but not before sharing her suspicions with one of her friends.

It wasn't long before that friend said to those gathered around, "This fellow is one of them. He was with Jesus the Nazarene."

Some of the men chimed in and accused me of allegiance to Jesus. For a second time that night I denied my Lord. I said, "Man, I don't know what you're talking about." What was wrong with me? I was filled with anger and shame.

This double denial appeared to satisfy the crowd. They went on about their business, still buzzing about the events of that night. Things settled down. I thought perhaps—just maybe—I had fooled them all. Two denials surely would be enough to save my neck, but I was wrong.

The night dragged on. What was happening in that hearing hall? What were they doing to Jesus? About an hour later a man came to me and said, "You're a Galilean, aren't you?" I knew my speech identified me from the north country, but so what? Many Galileans were in town for the Passover. What was he getting at? Were these people still trying to link me with Jesus? In desperation I said, "Man, I don't know what you're talking about." Angry and excited, I began to call curses down on myself and swear that I never knew Jesus. What a pathetic sight I must have been.

But my tirade was interrupted when a rooster began to crow. It was just as Jesus predicted. He told me I would deny him three times before the cock crowed. I said it could never happen, but it did.

I, His ardent follower and chief defender—I had become the voice of denial. The crowing of the cock was proof. It meant nothing to the others, only that the morning had arrived. To me, it meant everything.

Now I stand here disgraced and despondent. I couldn't even admit that I know Jesus. What kind of a disciple am I?

Perhaps one day Jesus will give me the opportunity to show how I really feel about Him. Perhaps I can declare my love just as much as this night I denied it. For now, the shrill crowing of that rooster rings in my ears. It's a sound I'll never forget; it's a sound I pray Jesus does not remember.

Chief Priests

VOICES OF DECEPTION
Matthew 27:62-66; 28:11-15

RRG

THE CHIEF PRIESTS, VOICES OF DECEPTION

here is no deception so subtle as self–deception. The chief priests thought they could deceive the world about the true nature of Jesus—and for many they did. But in the end they most deceived themselves in thinking they could thwart God's plan of salvation.

My name is Abishua. My friends and I are chief priests in Jerusalem. We've taken over the functions of the temple, and, together with the scribes, we are the most powerful religious leaders in Jerusalem.

As the worship leaders of Israel, our authority is unquestioned. Everyone knows of our lineage. From the time of Aaron until now, we are God's chosen vessels, His official ministers. We, and we alone, represent the people to Jehovah. There is no room for discussion on this subject, and we have no time for interlopers.

That's why this situation with Jesus riled us so much. His teachings disrupted the people, not to mention our temple practices. He was a radical; the people must have nothing to do with Him.

There have been others before Him of course, but none as dangerous. His followers were growing in number and becoming more militant in their belief that He was our long–awaited Messiah. We could not tolerate this threat to our authority. Something had to be done, and we were the people to do it.

Jesus of Nazareth came on the scene rather quickly. The crowds were small when He was baptized in the Jordan River by John, that nonconformist. But those crowds swelled to hundreds, thousands in some cases. We had to stop this man.

We plotted His death for months. Are you surprised? Does it disturb you that the ministers of the house of God would plan the execution of a rival? Don't be surprised. On the surface we may carry ourselves with a dignified air, but we are not immune to the vengeful and pitiful attitudes that plague our hearts. Let me put it bluntly— we wanted Him dead. We thirsted for Jesus' blood.

He healed a man with a withered hand on the Sabbath; how dare He claim to be Lord of the Sabbath? He came to Jerusalem and drove those who changed money out of the temple, something we should have done ourselves. He made fools out of us. He taught in parables not always understood by the crowds, but we knew He was talking about us.

Yes, our plot to kill Him had been in the works for a long time. When one of His followers came to us and offered to betray Him, we saw our chance to get rid of this troublemaker. The traitor's name was Judas, a man of Cheroth, and he was tired of all the talk about love and forgiveness. It was evident he hated Jesus—perhaps not as much as we did—but he hated Him nonetheless. For just thirty pieces of silver he would hand Him over to us. It was a bargain. The plot began in earnest.

We had just finished our meal when Judas knocked at the door. He came directly from a room where Jesus and His followers were gathered. Judas told us that soon they would leave that room and likely go out the Eastern Gate to the Garden of Gethsemane. The clock was ticking, and the details of our Passover plot began to take shape.

Judas led us to the garden, where he kissed Jesus in an act of betrayal. We commanded that Jesus be bound and taken to the house of the high priest. There He received a pre–trial hearing by Annas and later stood before Caiaphas to answer the accusations we leveled against Him.

My friends and I engineered this "trial" very carefully. We knew we had no legitimate charge against Jesus, so we paid false witnesses to testify. They all condemned Him as deserving of death. Members of the Sanhedrin agreed. Well, all but a few—Joseph tried to say a few words in Jesus' defense, but only weakly. Our plan was working perfectly.

The high priests took Jesus to Pilate, the governor, for sentencing and punishment. We went along to add legitimacy to our trumped–up charges. Pilate would have to believe us. He had no other choice. We knew he despised us, as we did him, but we hated Jesus even more.

It was daybreak when we arrived at the governor's residence. We clamored for a hearing. Sleepy–eyed and disinterested, Pilate nonetheless listened to our charges. He repeatedly took the position that Jesus had done noth-

THE CHIEF PRIESTS, VOICES OF DECEPTION

THE CHIEF PRIESTS, VOICES OF DECEPTION

ing wrong. This would not do; we wanted Him dead. We had paid a disciple to betray Him. We had paid witnesses to lie about Him. We had come too far; we could not turn back now.

We sprinkled ourselves throughout the crowd waiting for Pilate's decision. When he appeared, we who raised our voices in deception now raised them in defiance. "Crucify Him, crucify Him!" With those words we began a chant that rippled through the crowd. Jesus must die. We had spent too much time on our plot. We couldn't let Him get away now.

Our plan worked. Pilate released Jesus to the crowd. He was taken by Roman soldiers to the place of the skull, where they crucified Him as a common criminal. We felt a sense of accomplishment. Then something happened.

Pilate wrote a sign to place on the cross above the head of Jesus. The governor wrote it in Aramaic, Latin and Greek so everyone could read it. The sign said, "Jesus of Nazareth the King of the Jews."

We immediately objected. "Don't write, 'the King of the Jews.' Write instead that He said, 'I am King of the Jews.'" But Pilate stiffened his resolve and he refused.

We got Jesus to the cross, but somehow I sensed that He had beaten us. We were gleeful; He was genuine. We were horrible; He was honorable. We were vicious; He was victorious. When we lifted Him up, we put ourselves down.

There were many voices raised in Jerusalem that infamous day, but none so deceptive as ours. Sometimes I hate being a chief priest.

Caiaphas

VOICE OF CONDEMNATION
Matthew 26:59-68

RRG

CAIAPHAS, VOICE OF CONDEMNATION

Not all those who wield power hold office. Caiaphas was the high priest at the time of Christ's arrest, but he was really only a puppet for his father–in–law, Annas. Because of family ties and other practical reasons, Caiaphas chose to do what others wanted rather than what was right. In the process his voice condemned an innocent man to death.

I remember that night so clearly. A mob burst into the courtyard of my home. They had a man whom they had arrested and bound. Their first stop was at the residence of Annas, my father–in–law. I was used to that. It hardly bothered me anymore.

Whenever my countrymen had a quarrel against anyone, they came to me for a hearing, but not before they saw Annas. Governor Quirinius appointed my father–in–law as high priest for nine years. When a new governor took over, Annas was dismissed. That took place more than fifteen years ago, but he was still the dominant member of the Jewish hierarchical machine. Annas is a clever manipulator and a ruthless opponent. I wouldn't want to be on his bad side. I've been called rude,

sly and hypocritical, but I'm no match for my father–in–law. I know that. I have the office, but he has the power.

The man this angry mob brought that night was Jesus of Nazareth. I had heard of Him. He was an itinerant preacher. Some said He was a prophet. A rumor even floated around that He might be the Messiah. I considered the whole matter rubbish.

It was late—about midnight— and I had already gone to bed. Apparently Annas was still up. He spent just enough time with the prisoner to allow me to get dressed and come down to the hall, where I would greet the chief priests. By this time the elders of the city and some members of the Sanhedrin had arrived. They told me that Jesus of Nazareth was a blasphemer and His case needed my immediate attention. I wasn't much interested in the whole affair, considering it was the middle of the night. Still, I agreed to hear their complaint.

Our hurriedly called meeting convened a few minutes later. The Sanhedrin heard the evidence against Jesus. It was pretty flimsy stuff. His preliminary interview with my father–in–law turned up nothing that really incriminated Him either. We decided we needed more proof if the charge was to stick. Besides, in our haste, not all the members of the Sanhedrin were present.

I decided to adjourn this inquisition and renew it several hours later. Frankly, I wished He would just go away. Since that wasn't likely to happen, I commanded my men to take Jesus down to the dungeon in the lowest level of my house. There, in those dank, dark quarters He would be held in chains until the evidence could be gathered.

In the morning, shortly before dawn, we reconvened. All the council members were present, in addition to the elders of the people, the chief priests and the scribes. Witnesses were brought forth who claimed they heard Jesus make blasphemous statements, but they could not agree on what He said. Their stories were filled with holes and contradicted each other. Obviously, their testimony wasn't going to convict anyone. The trial was quickly turning into a fiasco.

Then one member of the Sanhedrin asked Him, "If you are the Christ, tell us."

There. The question had been put to Jesus directly. His response was not as direct. He said, "If I tell you, you will not believe." Then He said something about the Son of Man being seated at the right hand of God. That enraged the Sanhedrin. One of them asked, "So you are the Son of God?" This time His reply was very direct: "I am."

The crowd became incensed. They tore their clothes and began to shout invectives at Him. "Blasphemer!" "Traitor!" "Pagan!" Yet to every charge He stood silent. Some struck Him with their fists and spat upon Him. He remained unmoved. I was awestruck by His composure.

While the Sanhedrin worked itself into a frenzy, fear and uncertainty gripped my heart. Whatever these men might think, I knew this whole affair was wrong. How did we expect to get away with it? This was not a trial. It was a sham. Our law does not permit a trial to be held at night, and yet we had been up all night long trying to find evidence against Jesus. Furthermore, we all knew that the whole situation came about because of blood money paid to one of Jesus' followers. We even asked the defendant to incriminate Himself, which our law excluded. Now they expected me to pass a sentence of death, and yet I knew that it could not be done legally until the day after the accused was convicted. What were we thinking? How would this farce be viewed in years to come?

My father–in–law was watching me. I could feel his steely stare piercing right through me. I knew I had been elected high priest only because of his power and influence. Would I follow his wishes and please the chief priests, or would I rise to a higher sense of justice and throw this case out? I had no choice. This Jew meant nothing to me; my father–in–law, everything.

Yes, I am one of the twelve voices of Easter. Mine is the voice of condemnation. It was my voice that proclaimed this innocent Nazarene guilty of blasphemy. What else could I do?

Pilate

VOICE OF EVASION
Matthew 27:11-26

RRG

*E*vade the issue. Avoid the confrontation. Take the path of least resistance. Such actions may work with politics but not with Jesus. Pilate learned too late that not to decide for Jesus is to decide against Him.

It was springtime in Jerusalem, time to shake the winter of this barren wasteland out of my bones. If I could only get through the Passover festival. If these Jews would just let me alone and cause me no problems during their week of celebration, then I could return home to my palace in Caesarea and breathe the sea air wafting in from the Mediterranean. Perhaps this spring would be different. Perhaps the Jews would not be such a problem to me.

I've never been popular with these people, and I really don't care. Everything about them annoys me, particularly their religious convictions and their stubborn pursuit of tradition. Often I've done things just to anger them, to make their lives as miserable as they have made mine. Still, I journeyed to Jerusalem. I wanted to make sure these pesky people didn't get out of hand during Passover.

It was early Friday morning, just after sunrise. I saw the Sanhedrin, the chief priests and elders coming toward my quarters. They looked especially agitated that day. The only one who seemed calm and at peace was the man they brought in bonds with them. That man was Jesus of Nazareth, whom the religious leaders accused of misleading the Jewish people, encouraging them not to pay taxes to Caesar and claiming to be their Messiah. I thought it ironic. These Jews, who hated paying taxes to Rome, were charging one of their own with encouraging nonpayment of taxes.

The man stood meekly in front of me. I asked if He was really the King of the Jews. I wanted everyone to hear the sarcasm in my voice. I wanted them to know how ridiculous I thought this whole situation was. But I wasn't ridiculing Him; I was ridiculing the Sanhedrin and the chief priests.

It was evident this man had committed no serious crime, and I told the Jewish leaders that. Still, they insisted that He stirred up the people, especially in Galilee. Troublemakers always seemed to come from Galilee.

PILATE, VOICE OF EVASION

I did not want to deal with Jesus, and when I heard that He was from Galilee, I saw the opportunity to slither out of my responsibility. Galilee was under the jurisdiction of Herod Antipas, who happened to be visiting Jerusalem. Immediately I sent this band of angry priests to him. I hated Herod almost as much as I hated the Jews, and I was glad to get rid of my problem by creating one for him.

Unfortunately my joy was short–lived. Herod wanted to see Jesus because he heard He had performed many miracles. But soon he began to mock this Nazarene and deride Him, as did the others. He put a gorgeous robe around Him and with a contemptuous laugh sent the prisoner back to my judgment hall.

Again the chief priests and rulers looked to me for a judgment. I did everything possible to evade the issue. They were crying for Jesus' blood. I didn't think they had the courage to insist on crucifixion, so after another examination I presented my findings a second time. "I find nothing in this man to substantiate the charges you bring against Him. Nothing He

has done deserves the death penalty." Defiantly, they refused to accept my verdict.

That irritated me. I wanted to shake off this case. I wanted it behind me. I tried to return Jesus to the Sanhedrin, but that did not work. I attempted to force Herod to deal with Him, but that failed too. Finally I proposed a compromise.

In the past I released a prisoner to the Jews each year at Passover. While I hated them, deep down I really feared them, and this release usually placated them. I wanted to release Jesus this year, but the chief priests wouldn't have it. They incited the crowd to cry for Barabbas, a thief and a murderer, instead of Jesus. I couldn't believe my ears. How much they must have hated Him! Again my efforts to evade the issue failed.

I released Barabbas, but what should I do with Jesus? I thought if I beat Him—you know, roughed Him up a little—and then released Him, surely that would satisfy the Jews. I ordered Jesus scourged, beaten with a whip of thongs. Each thong was tipped with pieces of lead or brass or even sharp bits of bone to make it more painful. My soldiers stripped His back bare and began to flog Him. The lashes exposed deep–seated veins and arteries. It was a cruel beating, but better than being crucified. Surely this would satisfy those blood–thirsty priests.

But it didn't. I presented Jesus to the howling mob, expressing for the third time my serious doubts that He was guilty of anything worthy of death. Despite this the crowd began to yell, "Crucify Him, crucify Him, crucify Him!" Their stubborn insistence made me tremble and quiver. Surely this man Jesus deserved better.

I knew what was right. I knew what I needed to do, but I lacked the courage to do it. I just wanted to get all this behind me. It appeared the only way was to release Jesus to the crowd. Calling for a basin of water, I washed my hands of Him and turned Him over to the mob. They put a cross on Jesus' back and led Him out of the city to Skull Hill.

It's all over now. I thought I could remain neutral about Jesus, but it was impossible. When you encounter this man, you have to choose one side or the other. I fear I chose the wrong side.

I gave in to the intimidation of the chief priests. I wavered. I didn't have the courage to do what was right. I should have raised my voice, and I did. But mine was the voice of evasion. As a politician I was used to compromise, but this wasn't compromise. This was cowardice.

Voices of Hatred
Matthew 27:15-26

RRG

Hate has a thousand faces, but all of them are ugly. The mob that stood before Pilate's judgment hall was filled with such an ugly hatred one could feel it in the air. And in the name of hate, the Lord of glory was condemned to die.

We're not proud of it, but we were part of the mob that dreadful weekend. Jews were in town from all over to celebrate the Passover. But there was a sense of expectation in the crowd, an expectation that something out of the ordinary was going to happen. Little did we realize how extraordinary the events of that week we're going to be. Here's our story.

We were milling around in the streets late one night when we saw some priests hurrying to the Roman fortress of Antonio. There was evil in their eyes and murder on their minds. They picked up a detachment of soldiers and headed toward the eastern perimeter of the city. We wanted to see what was going on, so we followed them.

It was dark. The only light available was the torches the mob carried. When we arrived at Gethsemane we saw Him, the One these chief priests were looking for, Jesus of Nazareth. He didn't appear very sinister to us. In fact, He had been praying in the garden. He came to us with greetings of peace. We came to him with torches and swords and clubs.

Quickly they arrested Jesus and whisked Him away to the palace of the high priest. During the trek across Jerusalem's dark streets we decided to back off and leave the mob. We simply ducked into one of the dimly lit alleys.

The next day there was a ruckus in the street outside the fortress. The mob had re-formed, and we wanted to see what was happening. We joined them in front of the governor's judgment hall. There stood Pilate himself with Jesus. He was beaten and bloodied. Still, He had a face of quiet confidence and a deep look of compassion in His eyes.

Pilate addressed the mob, "I find no fault in this man. What do you want me to do with Him?" Then things turned cruel. The chief priests began to cry, "Crucify Him! Crucify Him!" The crowd picked up the chant. It was loud and sinister. "Crucify Him! Crucify Him! Kill

Him! He deserves to die." Their anger was so infectious that we found ourselves hating a man we did not even know.

Finally, Pilate delivered Jesus of Nazareth to the crowd. We made Him bear His cross out of the city to Golgotha. What a pathetic sight. Our hatred swelled as He made His way through the narrow streets. He was beaten so badly and had lost so much blood that He could hardly stand. Then He collapsed beneath the weight of the cross. The Roman soldiers commanded a Cyrenian named Simon to carry it for Him. We all shouted obscenities against Jesus. Who did He think He was anyway? The king of the Jews? The Son of God? What gave Him the right to claim that?

What a mixed mob we were. Men like us cursed the man who was to be hung on the cross. Roman soldiers struggled to maintain crowd control. The chief priests and Pharisees paraded self–righteously through the streets in their long robes. Yet there were also some women who beat their breasts and lamented what was being done to Jesus. We could tell from their agonized cries they were His followers. But we

drowned out their calls to put an end to this brutality. Today we would have our way.

We finally arrived at the place the Romans call Calvary. Common criminals were crucified here, raised on crosses just barely off the ground and left to die. The soldiers nailed Jesus to the cross, stood it upright and dropped it with a jolt into a hole in the ground. You could hear the Nazarene sigh as the weight of His body pulled hard against the nails in His hands and feet. It was midmorning now—about 9 o'clock.

The crowd hurled jeers and taunts at Jesus. The Jewish religious leaders mocked Him. The Roman soldiers ridiculed Him. An oppressive hatred was in the air. How much we wanted Him to die; how pleased we were that His death was so painful.

But there was something different about this man. He spoke from the cross several times, yet never in anger or bitterness. He spoke to one of the thieves hanging next to Him. He spoke to a woman who appeared to be His mother and to a man with her. He made a request to the soldiers. He even appeared to direct some comments toward heaven. I thought I heard Him say something about His Father forgiving us. How could He pray for our forgiveness after what we had done to Him? How could He return our hatred with love?

We knew death was not imminent, so we all sat down. What a spectacle we must have been—sitting there, watching Jesus die.

Yes, we were among the twelve voices of Easter. We were the voices of hatred who cried, "Crucify Him! Crucify Him!" We ridiculed Him as He carried His cross out of the city. We even joined those who called for Him to come down from the cross and prove He was someone special. But when we were at our worst, He was at His best.

Hatred could not extinguish His love. Jesus was strangely determined to love us from that cross. He loved those who crucified Him. Perhaps we'll never understand why.

The Thief

VOICE OF FAITH
Matthew 27:44

THE THIEF, VOICE OF FAITH

*L*ord, remember me when you come into Your Kingdom." Hardly the words one would expect from a thief. Yet, spoken in faith, they brought forgiveness for the past, peace for the present and hope for the future to a dying man.

It was clearly the turning point in my life. Granted, there wasn't much time left; in hours this cross would wrench the life from me. Yet if I were to live a hundred more years I would never look into a kinder face than that of Jesus of Nazareth. I truly believe that He is the Christ.

I heard many things about Him, but His calm, majestic manner— even on the cross—drew me to Him. I can't explain it. I don't understand it totally myself. I've never trusted anyone in my life, but here I am trusting a man about to die. Ridiculous, you say? Let me tell you my story.

I never had an easy life. I grew up stealing, cheating and conning people. I started when I was a boy—only eight or nine. I'd run through the streets, snatching fruit from the vendors or wares from the shops. It all seemed innocent at first; it was just a game. But by the time I was a teenager I was really good at my craft. I was a professional thief.

Over the years I learned to trust nothing except my ability to steal from others. I would cheat anyone, anytime, anyplace. As I saw it, if I did not steal I would have nothing. I had no intentions of going through life with nothing, so I stole.

As I grew older my crimes became more serious. I even stole from some of the Roman soldiers. It was always a thrill. My head swelled with pride knowing that I could get away with it. I hated them anyway. I figured whatever I took from them, they owed to me. They took taxes and anything else they wanted from our people, so I was just getting back a little of our own. But I hated my people too. The Jews had done nothing for me except cause trouble. What I stole from them, they owed me as well.

Oh sure, I was caught many times, but always let go. This was the first time they took my petty crimes so seriously. Perhaps the judge saw my face one too many times. So here I hang, condemned to die.

I didn't really know the other two who were hanging on crosses with me. I had heard of the one on the middle cross, Jesus. Some people thought He was the Messiah. Others said He was a magician—that He raised people from the dead. I didn't really know who He was and I didn't much care until . . .

We had all been physically beaten but especially Him, the one in the middle. The soldiers paid particular attention to Him. I heard them mocking and ridiculing Jesus. I had nothing to lose, so I joined in. So did the other guy hanging on the far cross. Isn't it ironic? Here we were mocking the One hanging between us, and we were about to die ourselves.

I watched Him. I noticed how He responded to the scoffing. He made no retort—not a word. Why didn't He show any anger? Why didn't He curse us as we cursed Him? I couldn't believe how calm and peaceful He was.

Gradually, my jeers turned to silence. I didn't know what to say. This Jesus amazed me. I found myself rebuking the man on the other side of Him. Indignantly I said, "Don't you fear God? Don't you see that we are being punished justly for our crimes, but this man has done nothing wrong? How can you continue to ridicule Him?"

It just didn't seem right. Jesus didn't belong here, hanging between two thieves like us. We were criminals, but He looked so innocent. I believe He was innocent. In fact, I began to think that maybe He was who He claimed to be—the Christ, the Son of the living God.

With this tiny bit of faith I turned to Him, looked squarely into His face and said, "Lord, remember me when You come into Your kingdom."

I couldn't believe I was saying this, but I knew in my heart He had to be the Lord. If that was true, then everything He said about His kingdom was also true. All I wanted was for Him to remember me when He became our king. I was surprised when He said, "Today you will be with Me in paradise."

What did He mean, *paradise*? That didn't sound like some mystical region of phantoms or some place to purge my sins. It sounded pretty real, and pretty good too. For that matter, what did He mean, *today*? I always believed that once you died that was it. Life just ended. Yet He promised me that on this day I would be with Him in paradise.

I trusted Him, this One hanging next to me on a cross. Even if I didn't understand everything, trusting Him made all the difference in the world. I became the voice of faith instead of doubt. For the first time I had faith in someone other than myself. For the first time I trusted someone with my life. For the very first time I had hope for the future, and all because of this man I met at Calvary.

Centurion

VOICE OF AFFIRMATION
Matthew 27:54

*oman soldiers were not known for their religiosity. Yet through the cross, Christ reached to the heart of an unknown centurion and changed his life. At the foot of the cross this man came to know that Jesus was truly the Son of God.*

The events of that weekend disgusted me. They exhausted me. But most importantly, they changed me.

I'm a Roman centurion—a non-commissioned officer with about a hundred men under my command. Sounds impressive, doesn't it? It's not. I'm just a grunt in the Roman army. I do whatever I'm told.

It all began when my commander sent word to our barracks. It was late at night, and the Jews were at the Antonio Fortress. They wanted Roman soldiers to accompany them to arrest a traitor. My commander told me to take my men and go with them.

We left the Tower of Antonio and went east out of the city to the olive garden. What an entourage. We were led by a Jewish informant named Judas. He was followed by

angry chief priests and scribes. Their temple police were with them, and my men brought up the rear. We pierced the darkness with swords and clubs and torches. Though the air was brisk, it was heavy with hatred.

When we arrived at the garden called Gethsemane, a man came forward and asked, "Whom are you seeking?"

Our informant stepped forward and, in an act of apparent friendship, gave the man a kiss. This was our signal. Still, I thought it best to confirm the identification, so I responded, "Jesus of Nazareth."

"I am He," the man replied.

His frank admission so overwhelmed us that we lurched backward and many of my men fell. I arrested Jesus and led Him away to the house of the high priest. I thought I would never see Him again, but I was wrong.

Later that night the Jews took Him to Pilate's judgment hall at the Antonio Fortress. They already had held some kind of a trial and convicted Jesus. They demanded that Pilate sentence Him to death.

I could see that Pilate was going to waver on this one. He

didn't believe Jesus had done anything worthy of death, but spineless as he was, he refused to take a stand and free Him. Instead, he instructed me to have Him flogged. I gave the nod, and happily my men obliged.

They scourged Him mercilessly, opening His back with deep and hideous wounds. My men were enjoying it far too much. They mocked Jesus because He had said He was king of the Jews. One of them found some nearby thorns and made a crown of them. I winced as I saw them push it into His tender brow. They slapped Him, spat upon Him, ridiculed Him. They probably would have killed Him, but that was reserved for something even more diabolical—the cross.

My soldiers led Jesus away and made Him carry His cross from Antonio to a small hill outside the city wall. We call it Calvary; the Jews call it Golgotha. There they nailed Him to the cross and dropped it into a hole. He hung just a few feet off the ground.

The chief priests continued mocking Jesus. They said, "If you're really who you claim to be,

come down from that cross and save yourself." My men chimed in, "Yeah, if you're the king of the Jews, save yourself." I've never seen so much hatred targeted toward one person.

I had followed the brief career of this Nazarene. The authorities thought He was a troublemaker, so they told me to keep an eye on Him. So far as I know, He never did anything wrong. That's why I can't say that I was proud of what my men did to Him. Oh, I didn't really believe He was the Messiah or the Son of God. I thought He was just a deluded fake. But nobody deserves to be treated the way He was treated.

During the hours He hung on the cross some odd things happened. The sky became dark, as black as at midnight. It was eerie. Someone said that the veil in the Jewish temple was ripped apart. But the soldiers I commanded seemed unshaken by these things. They were more interested in dividing up His clothes.

Still, there was something different about this man. His demeanor, His gentleness, His total—well, call it joy—at being crucified. I can't explain it. Once

THE CENTURION, VOICE OF AFFIRMATION

He looked toward heaven and I thought I heard Him say, "Father, forgive them, for they do not know what they are doing."

As the hours dragged on, I could see that His life was nearing an end. Again He looked upward and said something to heaven. Then He died.

After that some of the chief priests began to irritate me. They wanted me to hasten the death of the crucified because the Sabbath day was approaching. Jews don't permit bodies to hang on crosses during their holy day. The governor agreed and ordered me to break the men's legs. My soldiers did, but not Jesus' legs. It was evident there was no life left in His body. Just to make sure, however, I ordered one of my men to pierce His side with a spear. Water and blood gushed out. Jesus of Nazareth was dead.

What a weekend! We expected some trouble with so many Jews in town for their feast, but nothing like this. Who would ever believe these chief priests could hate a Jew the way they hated this Jesus? They accused Him of blasphemy, but I saw no blasphemer die on the cross that day.

Yes, I'm one of the twelve voices of Easter. Usually I am the voice of authority. Today I was the voice of affirmation. Jesus was who He claimed to be. Almost inaudibly and with inexpressible wonder I said, "Certainly this was a righteous man."

I don't know what drew me to Him. Perhaps it was the promise I heard Him make to the thief hanging beside Him. Jesus told him that he would be with Him in paradise. I wish He had said that to me.

Joseph of Arimathea

VOICE OF COURAGE
Matthew 27:57-60

JOSEPH OF ARIMATHEA, VOICE OF COURAGE

*J*oseph of Arimathea was a secret follower of Jesus. From personal observation he was convinced that this itinerant preacher from Galilee was also the Messiah, the Son of God. It took Christ's death on the cross, however, for him to find the courage to boldly stand for what he believed.

I was there that night. It was a spectacle—a real circus. I had never seen the Sanhedrin so incensed. They were beside themselves with rage.

This was quite unusual for the Jewish high court. To begin with, we were hastily summoned to Caiaphas' house. Out in the courtyard were the temple police; inside were the judges and lawmakers of Israel. When I entered I was surprised to find standing before me a man I had come to know and admire: Jesus of Nazareth. In fact, I had concluded that He was the Messiah of Israel, the one we had so long awaited. Yet He was more.

I watched Him as He walked through the streets of Jerusalem. I heard Him teach in the temple. There was an air of authority about Him. The more I listened, the more I believed Him. He said He came to save those who were lost, and even though I was a respected member of the Sanhedrin, I knew that I was far from God. I embraced this man as my savior.

But I am not a brave man. I secretly followed Him because I was afraid the other members of the Sanhedrin would hear of my faith. If that happened, I stood a good chance of being put out of the council. What would a man my age do? I couldn't go back to Arimathea. There was nothing for me in that place. I would have no way to support myself. So while I believed that Jesus was indeed the Son of God, I never told anyone about it.

Now He stood before me. Angry voices derided Him, and false accusers lied about Him. Some of the Sanhedrinists raised objections with regard to the legality of this trial. I joined them and spoke timidly. But the majority ruled that day. They condemned my rabbi and sent Him to Pilate for what surely would be a sentence of death.

I was waiting for the kingdom of God as were many faithful Jews. I thought surely Jesus would repel the Roman invaders and establish that kingdom. Now my hopes were dashed. Pilate sent Him to the place of the skull, where they crucified Him. As He hung on the cross suffering so deeply, I stood in the shadows. I was too fearful even to draw near.

While Jesus was on the cross, however, a change took place in my heart. I saw Him with His arms outstretched, embracing all of humanity. I saw Him suffer and finally die for the sins of the world. I saw Him do the bravest thing I have ever seen. He could have come down from the cross and saved Himself from all that agony and pain, but He didn't. Perhaps it was His bravery that changed my voice of weakness to one of courage.

After the Roman soldiers pierced His side and determined that Jesus was dead, I left Golgotha and headed straight for the Tower of Antonio. I requested an audience with the governor. Because of my social position in the Jewish community, it was granted. In Pilate's presence I mustered enough courage to request that he release the body of Jesus into my custody. He was shocked to hear that Jesus was already dead. Since he never wanted to

have anything to do with this case anyway, he agreed to allow me to bury the body.

Quickly I found my friend Nicodemus and told him to meet me in an hour at my family tomb. I returned to Golgotha with Pilate's official written release. Presenting it to a centurion, who seemed to be shaken by the whole affair, I asked him to take Jesus' body down from the cross. He beckoned to his men and they quickly did so. With the help of some friends, we carried the body to my tomb nearby.

Nicodemus was already there. He had brought with him linen bandages, spices and aromatics—a mixture of myrrh and aloes. We did not embalm Jesus' body like the Egyptians do but simply wrapped it in layers of cloth and spices. It was late in the day and we needed to hurry. The Sabbath would soon be upon us, and we would have to cease working.

My family tomb was not a natural cave but rather man–made—one hewn out of solid rock. After we deposited Jesus' body in the tomb, Nicodemus and others helped me roll a great stone in front of the entrance. It was a heavy stone and would not easily be moved. Later, Pilate also sealed the tomb and commanded Roman soldiers to stand guard in front of it. The Jews wanted to make sure no one stole the body of Jesus.

I often wonder what gave me the courage to do what I did. I knew Roman law well enough to know that those condemned to death lost their right to be buried. I knew as well that Pilate hated the Jews, including all members of the Sanhedrin. But more than any-thing, I knew that this meant a complete break for me, a break with the Sanhedrin, a break with my culture and tradition, a break with the past. I was openly profess-ing before the entire world, includ-ing the Sanhedrin, that I was a believer in Jesus Christ. I had final-ly become the voice of courage.

In the face of sorrow, it was exhilarating to find the courage to lift my voice on behalf of my Savior. After all, He died for me; surely I could live for Him.

Mary Magdalene

VOICE OF ADORATION
Matthew 28:1-11

MARY MAGDALENE, VOICE OF ADORATION

Sorrow filled Mary's heart first at the cross and then at the tomb. The One who had changed her life, who had loved her as no one else ever had, was gone. Then one word changed it all, "Mariam." With that Mary knew her Master and Lord was alive. He was risen from the dead just as He promised. In adoration she worshiped the living Savior.

I knew Jesus for several years. I was frequently in the crowd when He taught about love, joy and peace. I watched Him raise the dead, heal the sick and cast out demons. But more importantly to me, He changed my life.

There were other women in our group whose lives He had changed. What a difference He had made for so many of us. Oh, we could not get as close to Him as His disciples—Peter, James, John and others—but we constantly felt the warmth of His smile and the gentleness of His voice. We knew He loved us as much as we loved Him.

Now it had all come down to this. I stood before His cross and watched Him die, His body racked with pain. I wept at the cruelty I witnessed. Those Roman soldiers were so inhumane. My people treated Him no better. The chief priests and scribes ridiculed Him; they hated Him so much. Yet Jesus said this was the hour for which He came to earth. All of us who saw Him through eyes of faith knew that He was laying down His life; these men were not taking it from Him.

Then the strangest thing happened. One of the members of the Sanhedrin appeared at the cross. I think his name was Joseph. He came from a town just twenty miles northwest of here. The man showed the centurion an official–looking paper from the governor that gave him permission to bury Jesus in his family tomb. The other women and I followed because we wanted to know exactly where they took Him.

We really wanted to prepare His body appropriately for burial, but the hour was getting late. The Sabbath began at sundown; we could not do anything more until it was over. We barely had time to do the essentials. My friends and I decided to return to the grave and finish our work as soon as the day of rest was ended. We loved

Him too much not to give Him a proper burial.

As soon as the Sabbath concluded the following evening and the bazaars reopened, Mary the mother of James, Mary the wife of Cleopas, Joanna, Susanna and others of us went into Jerusalem. We bought the spices necessary to anoint Jesus' body. Our plan was to go back to the tomb early the next morning.

The sun was just about to peak over the hills of Moab when we started out. We were far down the dark path to Joseph's tomb when we realized we forgot one important detail. Joseph closed the tomb with a huge stone. How would we ever move that stone? We nervously chatted about this as we hurried along. We agreed there must be a way. Someone said guards had even been posted at the tomb.

When we arrived at the tomb, however, we were shocked to see that the stone was not there, at least not over the entrance to the tomb. It had been rolled away—not simply rolled back but taken out of its trough and tipped over. It lay about a dozen feet from the tomb. There was no sign of the guards.

More surprises awaited us. While we stood puzzling over the mystery of the stone, two men suddenly appeared, dressed in dazzling white robes. These were not the togas of Roman soldiers, nor were they the long white robes of the Pharisees. In fact, I sensed these were not men at all; they were angels!

We were so frightened that we fell to the ground. The angels encouraged us by reminding us that Jesus said He would rise again. One of the angels told us to look inside the tomb. While the others did, I ran to tell Peter and John. Within minutes I returned with them, convinced that someone had stolen the body of Jesus. The linen garments were lying there neatly folded in their places, but the tomb was empty.

Peter and John and the other women quickly ran from the scene; I chose to remain behind in the garden. I was stunned. What had happened to my Savior? Where had He gone? Could it be that He did rise from the dead, or was His body just placed elsewhere by the soldiers? Who knew? I began to cry.

Then I heard a voice behind me ask, "Woman, why are you weeping?" I assumed it was the gardener. "Sir, what have you done with Him?"

Although now it was fully light, I could not see because tears blurred my eyes. He called my name. "Mariam." That was my Aramaic name, the name by which my parents and friends addressed me. A gardener would not have spoken Aramaic to me. Neither would a Roman. It could only be one person. I turned to my risen Lord and in adoration said,

"Rabboni." My heart filled with a sense of humble reverence. My Master, my Teacher, my Savior and my Lord stood before me alive!

Of course I am one of the twelve voices of Easter. How could I not be? It was Jesus. He was alive. He was risen from the dead. I was the first of His followers to raise my voice in adoration to the One who conquered death. I will not be the last. Thousands will follow. Come, let us adore Him, Christ the Lord.

Cleopas

VOICE OF ASSURANCE
Luke 24:13-40

*H*ope is one of the essentials of life. Two travelers from Emmaus began their journey home with no hope until they encountered a stranger on the road. In the end they came to know and share with others the hope that is in the resurrected Christ.

As the time to celebrate the Passover drew near, we traveled from our little village of Emmaus to Jerusalem. That's why we were in the capital when they crucified Jesus. When we left home, we never dreamed we would see anything like that. Our Savior, the only hope for the Jews and for the world, was put to death at a place called Skull Hill. I really believed this man was the Messiah. My friend and I even became His disciples. As we watched Him die, we knew He was gone forever, and so was our hope.

Of course we heard the rumor that He rose from the dead this morning, but we have no way of knowing for sure. Around Jerusalem rumors run rampant. We wished it were true, but we knew it couldn't be. Since nothing was left for us in Jerusalem, we decided to return home.

Our trip began somberly. Springtime was approaching, but we heard no birds singing, nor did we notice the flowers in the field. The skies were gray and bleak. We not only had buried our Savior, we had buried our hopes.

Slowly we trudged along in sad conversation. Then we heard footsteps behind us. I didn't recognize the man. When He came alongside, He noticed our sorrow and asked what we were talking about. At first neither my friend nor I responded. Finally I said, "Where have you been these last few days? Haven't you heard what's happened in Jerusalem? Are you a stranger to these parts?" I didn't see how anyone in the city could not know what had taken place.

Over the years, many people had been crucified. Since the Romans came, it was a rather common form of death. But never had there been a crucifixion like this one. A thick, inky darkness gripped the land for three hours. Earthquakes rocked the surrounding area. Some say that graves were opened and bodies were raised, appearing to people in Jerusalem. How could this stranger not know about these things? Yet He seemed sincere, so we told Him all that we experienced during the last three days. It was easy to talk to Him. He seemed almost like a friend.

We shared with Him that the One we believed would redeem Israel had been crucified. Our hopes had been dashed. Now no one would deliver us from the Romans. It had been three days since His burial. His body was already beginning to decay. Any tiny flicker of hope we might have had was swallowed up in a night of total despair.

We also mentioned how some of the women said they found the tomb empty this morning. Peter and John confirmed it. We had not personally seen the empty tomb, but we knew it couldn't be true.

Then our new companion spoke pointedly to us, "O foolish ones, and slow to believe all that the prophets have spoken! Christ had to suffer these things." He began to expound the Scriptures, beginning with Moses and the Prophets. Our ears quickened at what we heard.

We walked for hours as we listened to this man's teaching. By the time we arrived at our village it was late in the afternoon. We invited the stranger to stay with us. Traveling after dark was dangerous because of robbers. Besides, He was a remarkable person, and we wanted to hear more of what He had to say.

He accepted our invitation. We talked another hour or more. Soon it was time to eat. While we were reclining at the table, He took the bread, blessed and broke it, and we began to eat.

It was only then that I noticed the marks on His hands. I said, "Let me see Your hands." Slowly He turned them over, and there they were—nail prints. I raised my head and looked into His gentle eyes. My mouth dropped open; I couldn't say a word. My heart began to thump. I knew I was looking into the face of my blessed Redeemer, the risen Christ! The women were right after all! Peter and John were not talking nonsense. What Jesus predicted came to pass. He was alive and right here in my house, reclining at my table! No sooner did I understand who this divine stranger was than He disappeared.

I stood up quickly and said to my friend, "We've got to go back to Jerusalem. We have to tell them what has happened."

"Are you crazy?" he said. "We've just walked for hours, and it's after sunset. It will be dangerous."

He was right, but it didn't matter. We had to go back. We had to affirm what we had seen—that Jesus was alive.

We left everything behind and rushed to Jerusalem. That seven–mile journey was the most exciting trip of my life. I knew the disciples would be hiding from the authorities. We all feared the retaliation of Rome. We went to the secret rendezvous. Peter, James, John and many others were there. I could hardly wait to tell them.

I am one of the twelve voices of Easter. My name is Cleopas, the voice of assurance. Let others say what they will; I know it is true. Jesus is alive! I am an eyewitness to the resurrected Christ. I assure you, Jesus is alive!

Thomas

VOICE OF DOUBT
John 20:19-29

RRG

THOMAS, VOICE OF DOUBT

Doubt covered Thomas' face like a cloud on an otherwise clear day. How could he believe anything so miraculous as the resurrection? Was it wishful thinking? Was it a hoax? Graciously, Christ provided all the proof Thomas needed. In an instant his doubt turned to delight as he fell to his knees and worshiped his Lord and his God.

I can't forget that horrible scene at Golgotha: blood running down Jesus' face, His hands, His feet. Groans of agony escaping through the clenched teeth of those on either side of Him. The other disciples and I fled. We feared for our lives. We thought the Roman soldiers would come after us next, so we hid out in homes all over Jerusalem that night.

All the while I could think of only one thing—He was gone. He would never come back. Our plans were ruined. All of our hopes were shattered. I had never been so despondent in my life. Everything we worked for and dreamed about in the last three years was nailed to that cross. It was finished.

I loved Him. I was devoted to Him. I believed in Him. In fact, I was ready to die for Him. When the news came that Lazarus was dead and that Jesus was going to Bethany, I would not let Him go alone. I would go with Him even if it meant I would be killed.

His death should not have come as a surprise to any of us. He gave us little hints that this would happen one day. One time He said He would go away and prepare a place for us. None of us knew what He meant, so I said, "Lord, we don't know where you're going." I wasn't doubting His word; I just didn't understand. Jesus hinted about His death, but I guess we were all a little slow to catch on. Maybe we didn't want to admit that things might work out differently than we wanted. We planned to rule with Him over an earthly kingdom. A couple of the other disciples even asked to sit at His left hand and at His right. Now He was gone forever, and all those plans lay crumbled at our feet.

Then on the morning after the Sabbath, Peter and John and some of the women went to the tomb. They claimed it was empty and Jesus had risen from the dead. That night they met together in our

49

secret rendezvous, but I was not present. With Jesus dead, getting together seemed fruitless. According to those who were there, however, Jesus appeared! Throughout the next several days they repeatedly told me that Jesus was alive, but I would not believe.

I was so dejected that I dared not believe. Unless I could put my fingers in the nail prints in His hands, unless I could touch that horrible gash in His side, unless I could see Him and touch Him and have proof that He was alive, I could not believe. It's not that I didn't want to believe; I did. But I had to believe on my terms. Too often I had gotten my hopes up only to have them dashed. I wasn't going to be taken in again.

The other disciples continued to insist that they had seen Jesus alive. They offered their own witness as proof to me. But this was not the time for delusions fueled by wishful thinking; I needed to see for myself. I didn't want to hear about Him; I wanted to feel Him, to know for sure He was alive.

About a week later they all gathered at that same room. This time I was there. Much to our surprise, Jesus appeared in our midst. I knew He didn't come through the door; it was locked because we were all afraid. He greeted us, but none of us could respond. Then the most amazing thing happened. He spoke my name and said, "Thomas, put your finger here in the nail prints. Put your hand into the wound in my side and believe."

I was amazed, dumbfounded. Those were the exact demands I had made in order to believe. I had said it would be impossible for me to believe unless I could touch His hands and His side. Each thing I demanded He now commanded.

What more could I say? In one brief encounter He removed my doubt forever. This was unmistakably Jesus. I fell to my knees and said, "My Lord and my God."

I am one of the twelve voices of Easter. I admit I was the voice of doubt, but no longer. I want the world to know that my doubt evaporated like the morning dew.

If you doubt that Jesus is alive, if you doubt that He is God, doubt no longer. His words to me were a gentle rebuke. He said that I believed because I saw, but those who have not seen and yet believe are the ones truly blessed.

When you come face to face with the resurrected Christ, the voice of doubt, despair and despondency will be silenced. It must give way to the voice of faith and hope, because this Jesus is not a dead savior in some Jerusalem grave. He is the living Lord of glory!

I doubt no more. I have seen the resurrected Christ. The darkness of night has changed to the light of morning. Death is conquered by life. The Lord is risen indeed. This changes everything.